Other titles in the series:
The Crazy World of Aerobics (Bill Stott)
The Crazy World of Cricket (Bill Stott)
The Crazy World of Gardening (Bill Stott)
The Crazy World of Golf (Mike Scott)
The Crazy World of the Greens (Barry Knowles)
The Crazy World of the Handyman (Roland Fiddy)
The Crazy World of Hospitals (Bill Stott)
The Crazy World of Housework (Bill Stott)
The Crazy World of Learning to Drive (Bill Stott)
The Crazy World of Love (Roland Fiddy)
The Crazy World of Marriage (Bill Stott)
The Crazy World of the Office (Bill Stott)
The Crazy World of Photography (Bill Stott)
The Crazy World of Rugby (Bill Stott)
The Crazy World of Sailing (Peter Rigby)
The Crazy World of Sex (David Pye)

This paperback edition published simultaneously in 1992 by Exley
Publications Ltd. in Great Britain, and Exley Giftbooks in the USA.
First hardback edition published in Great Britain in 1989 by Exley
Publications Ltd.

Reprinted 1992. Third and fourth printings 1993.

ISBN 1-85015-353-1

Printed in Spain by Grafo S.A., Bilbao.

Exley Publications Ltd, 16 Chalk Hill, Watford, Herts WD1 4BN,
United Kingdom.
Exley Giftbooks, 359 East Main Street, Suite 3D, Mount Kisco,
NY 10549, USA.

the CRAZY world of CATS

Cartoons by Bill Stott

EXLEY

MT. KISCO, NEW YORK · WATFORD, UK

"*I think that hairdryer is too powerful for him...*"

"All that stuff about bringing them gifts – it's rubbish. We do it just to scare them!"

*"Oh come, come – does she look like a cat who'd
make a smell?"*

"O.K. a brief explanation will do. Why is my chicken leg in _your_ mouth?"

"An ultimate deterrent eh? Don't make me laugh fellas."

"*You must tell me if he's being a nuisance...*"

"How come _I_ get thrown out when the flea was found on the <u>carpet</u>?"

"You're sitting in his chair..."

"No more aimless yowling for us – I photocopied the words."

"Hey! There's wild life on this set!"

1

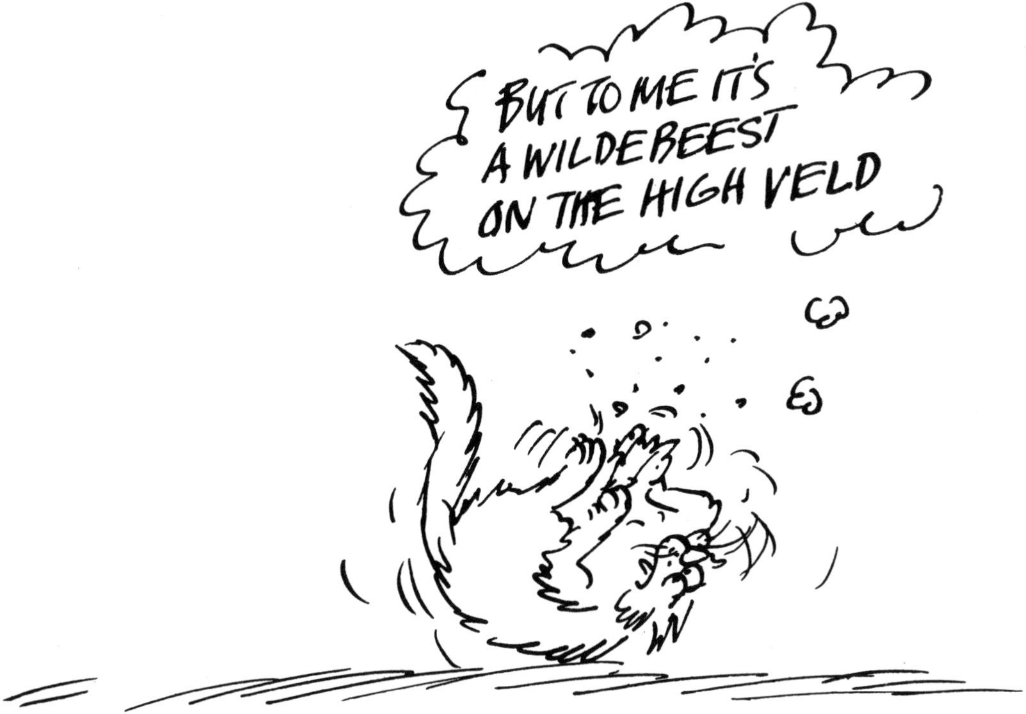
BUT TO ME IT'S A WILDEBEEST ON THE HIGH VELD

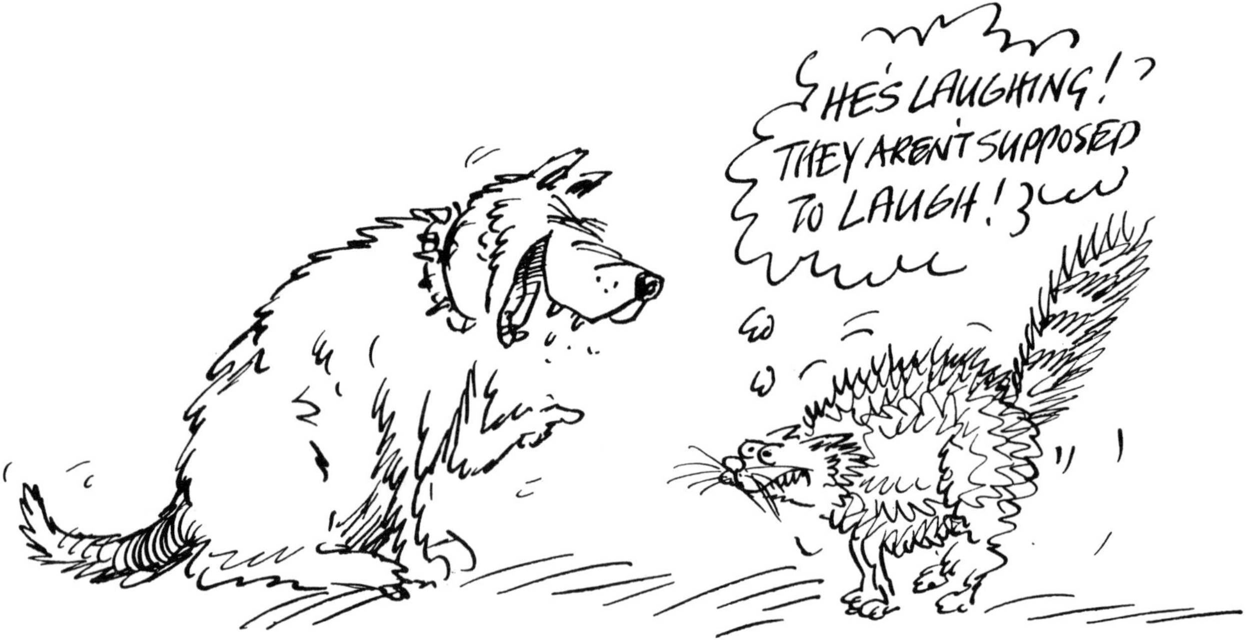
HE'S LAUGHING! THEY AREN'T SUPPOSED TO LAUGH!

"Gran! Oscar doesn't seem too keen on 'Kittichews'."

"*Have another go, Son – she's just playing hard to get...*"

"*Don't be alarmed. It's just his way of saying 'please don't hurt me.'*"

"Play with the yarn. Don't kill it!"

"What a coward! He's telling me the canary clawed the couch."

HELLO! IS MUMA'S DARLING PLEASED TO SEE HER?
OH MY GOD - THEY ATE GREEK AGAIN ~ THE GARLIC!

"This way I get all the excitement of the flying boot with none of the effort..."

"That's what I call a cat flap!"

"*Normally I'd have to admit you're a pretty hum-drum kind of guy. But with that can-opener in your hand, you're a giant.*"

"*Well, of course she's growling. You put ketchup on your
steak and she hates ketchup.*"

"The twins tried out your home perm kit on Chester."

"There are some _very_ distant relatives of yours on..."

"Since she stayed at the Hilton, she's become so fastidious…"

URRRRR...

1

2

"And when she actually deigns to come home, we'll do our tiger ambush!"

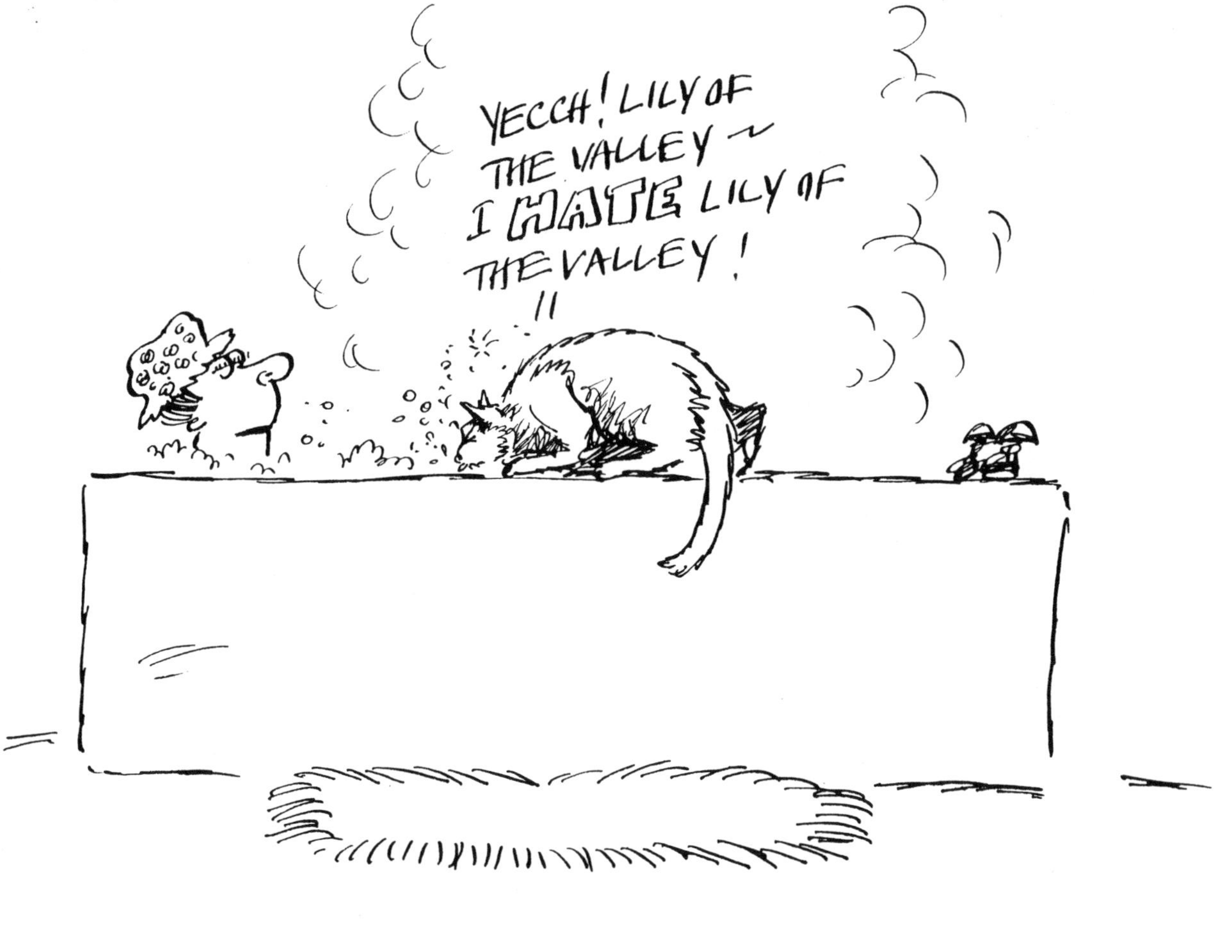
YECCH! LILY OF THE VALLEY ~ I HATE LILY OF THE VALLEY!

2

"It's as I suspected – the oaf doesn't speak Felinese!"

UH-UH~
HE KNOWS IT'S
CHEAP SOYA
SUBSTITUTE!
RIGHT FIRST TIME!
KITTY

"So much for your independence act!"

"What did the nasty man do to mama's little soldier?"

"I see that they still haven't fixed the spring on your catflap."

1

"You can tell he's a pedigree. He's the only member of the family who likes politics."

"*I can't teach her that she's not meant to bath in it!*"

"Remember the bird we nearly caught this morning? He's
back – with his big brother..."

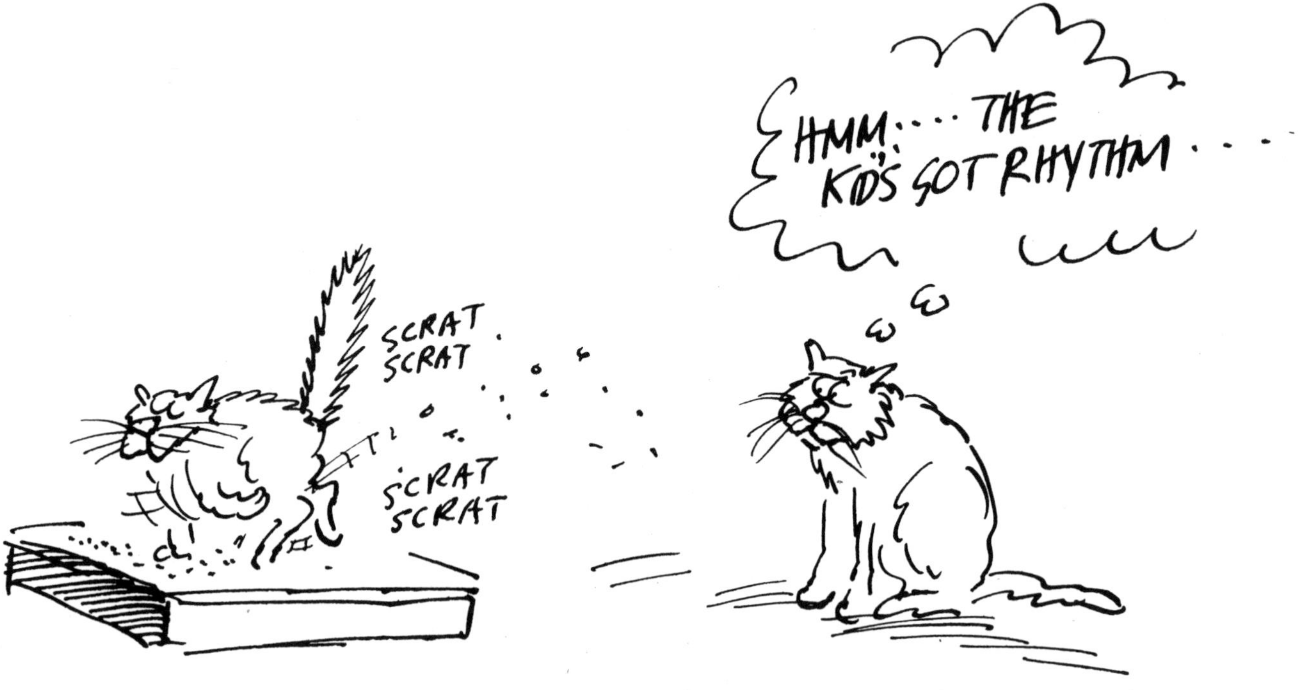
SCRAT
SCRAT
SCRAT
SCRAT
HMM.... THE KID'S GOT RHYTHM....

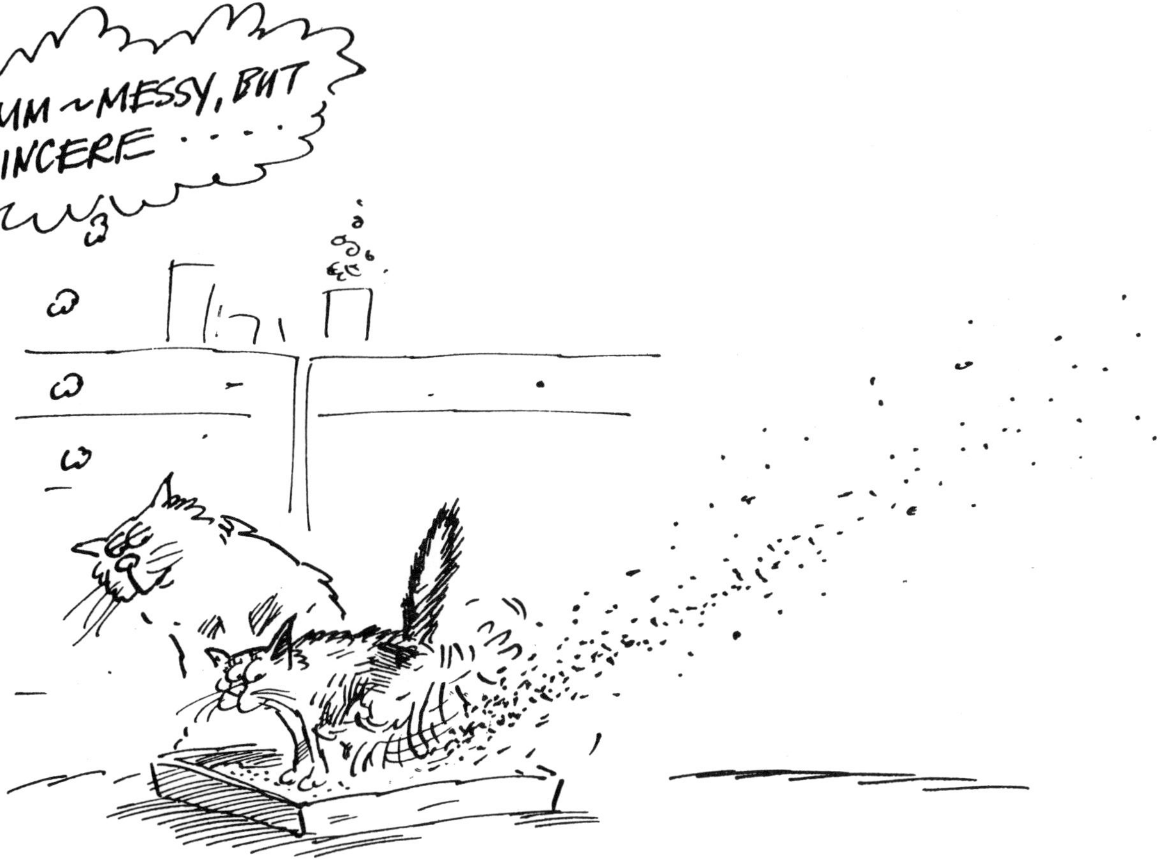
HMM ~ MESSY, BUT SINCERE . . . .

"Here Smelly, Smelly. Here Smelly..."

"So he's a little sharp – it beats all that yowling…"

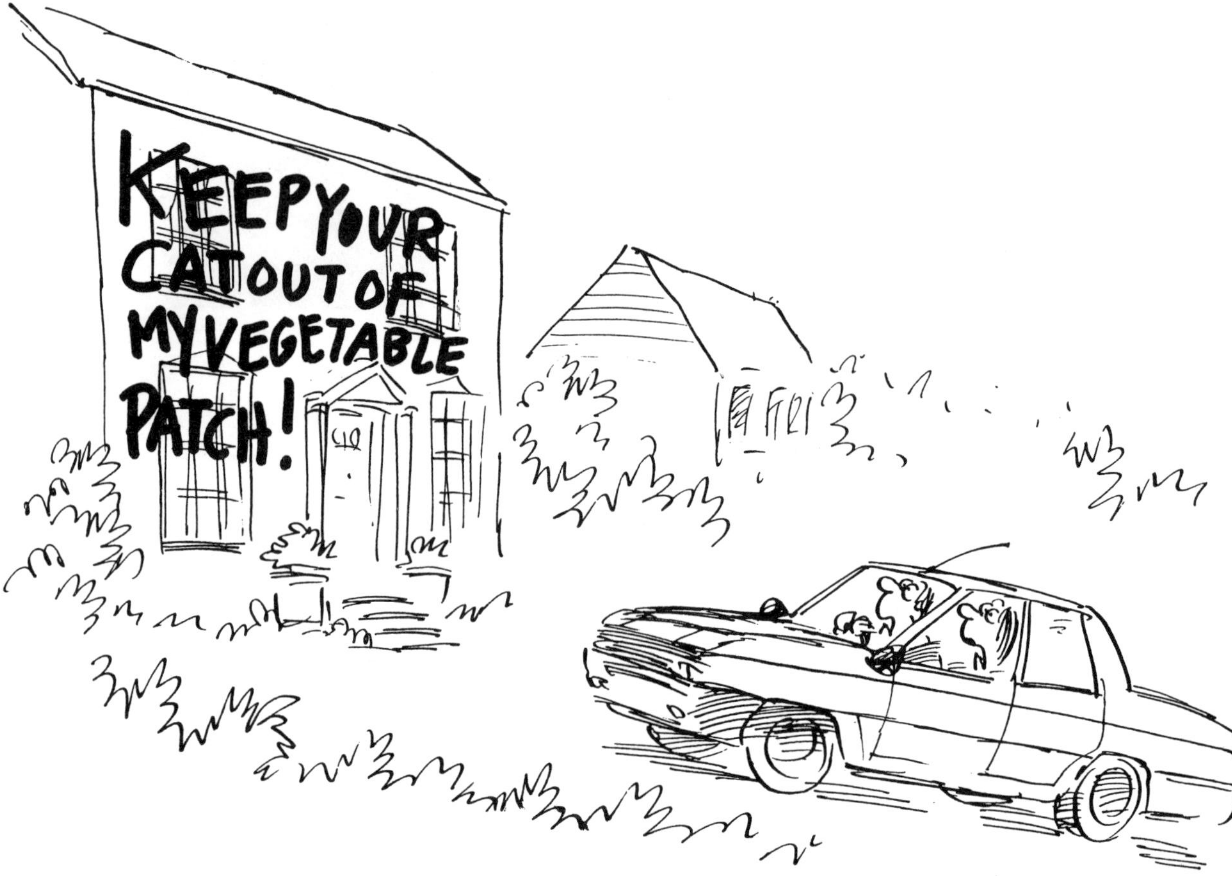
KEEP YOUR CAT OUT OF MY VEGETABLE PATCH!

COME ON RAMBO! DINSIE WINSIES!
SOMETIMES I THINK I MIGHT FIND MYSELF SOMEONE A LITTLE LESS EMBARRASSING!

1

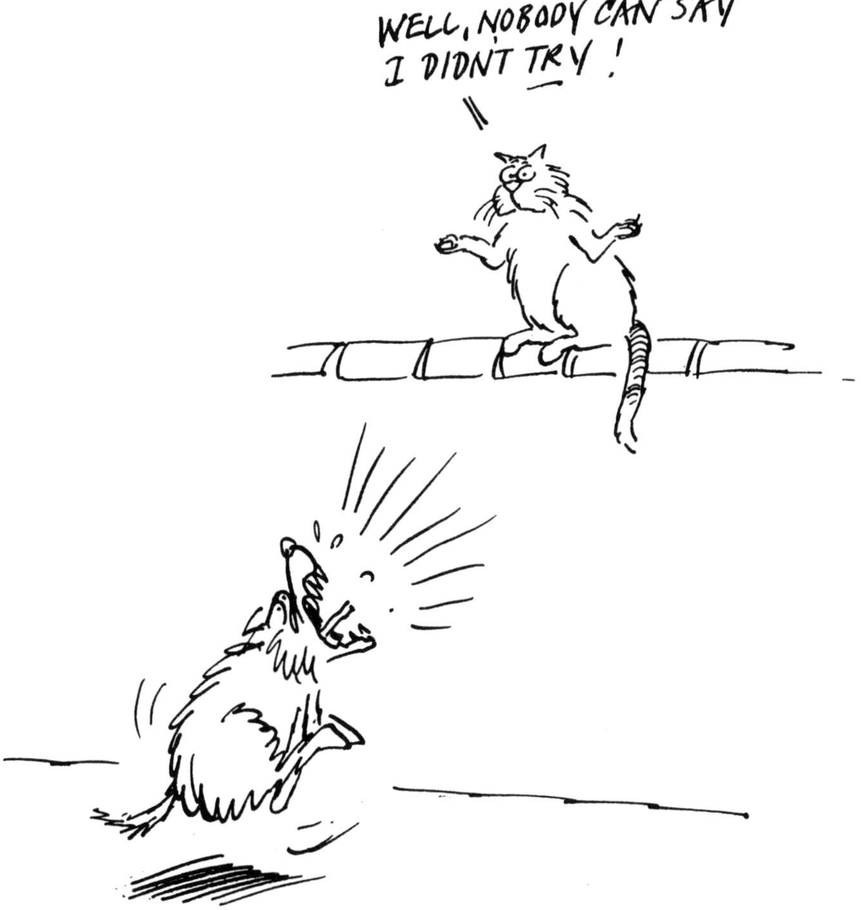
WELL, NOBODY CAN SAY I DIDNT TRY !

"Harold! Quick! The screens!"

"Don't worry about a thing – I had the operation..."

"*Learning to climb trees is cheating!*"

"Correct me if I'm wrong, but aren't we black cats supposed to be lucky?"

"What's wrong? He always washes that way – don't they all?"

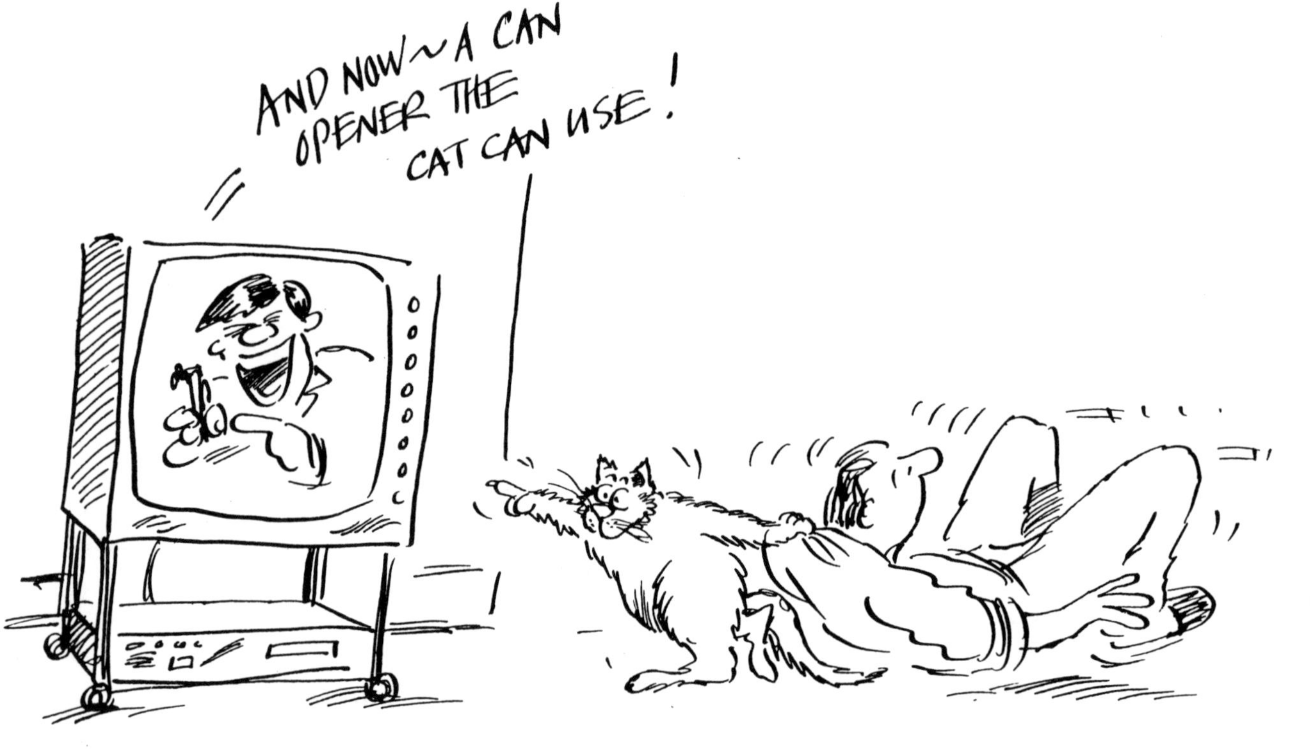
AND NOW ~ A CAN OPENER THE CAT CAN USE !

"… One of our regulars…"

1

*"Satisfy my curiosity – if you could get at me, would you
actually eat me?"*

"A simple 'yes' or 'no' will do."

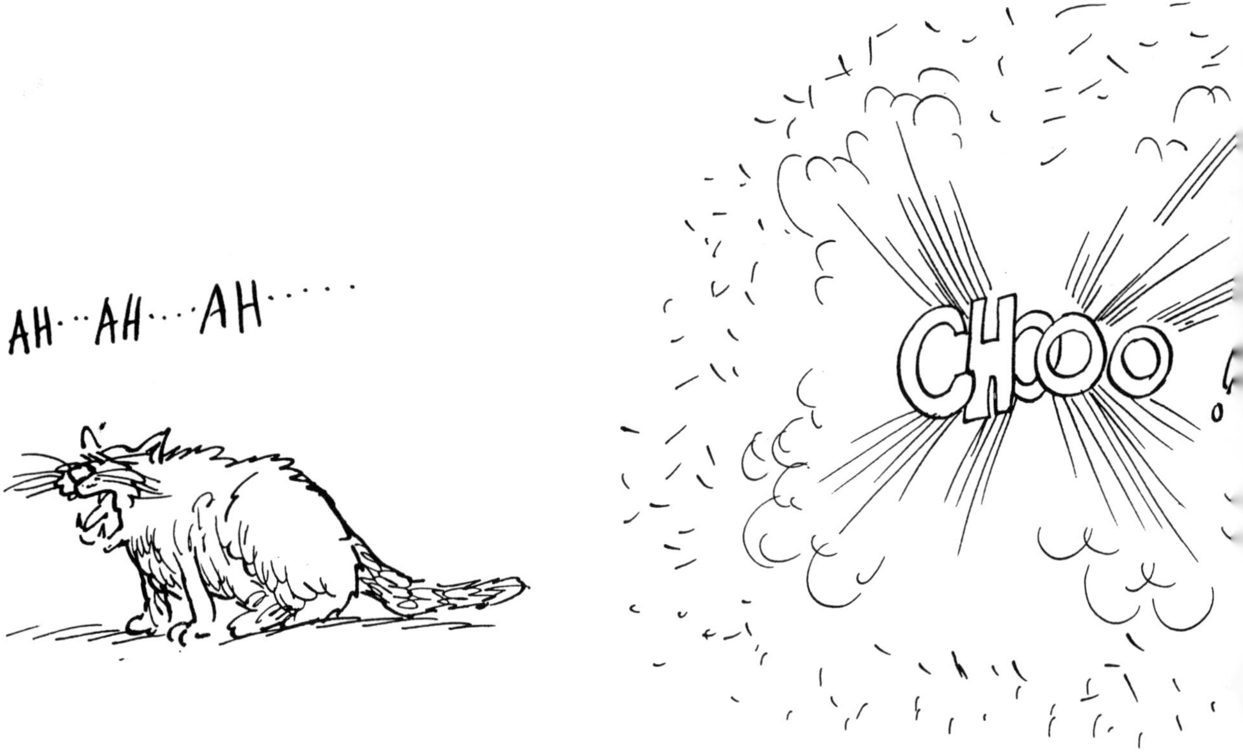
AH···AH·····AH······
CHOOO

"How many times do I have to tell you? Never change
channels without asking – it's very rude..."

*"Louie, I'd better hang up. They're staring at me the way
they always do when I use the 'phone."*

"Good, but not __that__ good – checkmate!"

"How'd you like it if I came and lay on your chest first thing in the morning?"

"I'll wait until someone comes by before I go and have a drink. I just love those cries of middle class outrage."

"Either you come in right now or you're out all night!"

Books in the "Crazy World" series

($4.99 £2.99 paperback)

The Crazy World of Aerobics (Bill Stott)
The Crazy World of Cats (Bill Stott)
The Crazy World of Cricket (Bill Stott)
The Crazy World of Gardening (Bill Stott)
The Crazy World of Golf (Mike Scott)
The Crazy World of the Greens (Barry Knowles)
The Crazy World of The Handyman (Roland Fiddy)
The Crazy World of Hospitals (Bill Stott)
The Crazy World of Housework (Bill Stott)
The Crazy World of Learning (Bill Stott)
The Crazy World of Love (Roland Fiddy)
The Crazy World of Marriage (Bill Stott)
The Crazy World of The Office (Bill Stott)
The Crazy World of Photography (Bill Stott)
The Crazy World of Rugby (Bill Stott)
The Crazy World of Sailing (Peter Rigby)
The Crazy World of Sex (David Pye)

Books in the "Mini Joke Book" series

($6.99 £3.99 hardback)

These attractive 64 page mini joke books are illustrated throughout by Bill Stott.

A Binge of Diet Jokes
A Bouquet of Wedding Jokes
A Feast of After Dinner Jokes
A Knockout of Sports Jokes
A Portfolio of Business Jokes
A Round of Golf Jokes
A Romp of Naughty Jokes
A Spread of Over-40s Jokes
A Tankful of Motoring Jokes

Books in the "Fanatics" series

($4.99 £2.99 paperback)

The **Fanatic's Guides** are perfect presents for everyone with a hobby that has got out of hand. Eighty pages of hilarious black and white cartoons by Roland Fiddy.

The Fanatic's Guide to the Bed
The Fanatic's Guide to Cats
The Fanatic's Guide to Computers
The Fanatic's Guide to Dads
The Fanatic's Guide to Diets
The Fanatic's Guide to Dogs
The Fanatic's Guide to Husbands
The Fanatic's Guide to Money
The Fanatic's Guide to Sex
The Fanatic's Guide to Skiing

Books in the "Victim's Guide" series

($4.99 £2.99 paperback)

Award winning cartoonist Roland Fiddy sees the funny side to life's phobias, nightmares and catastrophes.

The Victim's Guide to the Dentist
The Victim's Guide to the Doctor
The Victim's Guide to Middle Age

Great Britain: Order these super books from your local bookseller or from Exley Publications Ltd, 16 Chalk Hill, Watford, Herts WD1 4BN. (Please send £1.30 to cover postage and packing on 1 book, £2.60 on 2 or more books.)